157

R. Gibbo
65

THE FABER LIBRARY

OF ILLUMINATED MANUSCRIPTS

edited by Walter Oakeshott

The

Rohan Book of Hours

THE FABER LIBRARY OF ILLUMINATED MANUSCRIPTS

edited by Walter Oakeshott

THE ROHAN
BOOK OF HOURS

with an introduction and notes

by

JEAN PORCHER

FABER AND FABER LIMITED

24 Russell Square London

FIRST PUBLISHED IN MCMLIX
BY FABER AND FABER LIMITED
24 RUSSELL SQUARE LONDON WCI
PRINTED IN GREAT BRITAIN
BY WESTERN PRINTING SERVICES LTD, BRISTOL
COLOUR PLATES MADE AND PRINTED
BY FINE ART ENGRAVERS LTD, GUILDFORD
ALL RIGHTS RESERVED

Introduction

The art of illumination was the most widely practised of the pictorial arts north of the Alps in the first decades of the XV Century, and Paris was one of its main centres. To Paris artists flocked from every direction, not only men of true French stock, but also Mosans, Rhinelanders, Italians and others. What attracted them thither were the commissions of rich collectors, who vied with one another in the acquisition of their masterpieces, and the most opulent of whom took the finest of the artists into their personal service. About the year 1410, Jean, Duc de Berry, the King's uncle and a splendid patron of the arts, established in his household three young and gifted painters, Paul, John and Hermann called 'de Limbourg'. They had been summoned from Nimeguen by the Duke's brother, Philip of Burgundy, in 1402, and given an important artistic commission which was cut short by his death in 1404. In June, 1416, Jean de Berry himself died. The brothers Limbourg had died just before, and had been able to complete for him only one book, now known as the *Belles Heures*, which is in the Cloisters Museum in New York. This book, with its brilliant style and its daring innovations, was from the first an admired and coveted masterpiece; and when it came up for sale with the Duc's library, Yolande of Aragon, his niece by marriage, and like him seemingly a collector and lover of fine books, found herself fortunately placed, thanks to her husband's position, to secure it on favourable terms. For her husband was Louis II, King of Sicily and Duc d'Anjou, and was one of the executors of his uncle's will. The Queen borrowed the *Belles Heures* to examine. The book had been valued by experts at 700 *livres*, but she paid 300, and kept it.

The Queen of Sicily was not only a woman with some flair for business, as is obvious from the incident just described. She was also discriminating in her tastes, and she too maintained in her service an active *atelier* of illuminators. She commissioned from them, doubtless for her daughter Yolande (later the wife of Francis I, Duc de Bretagne) an important Book of Hours which subsequently belonged to Isabella Stuart, Francis's second wife, and is now in the Fitzwilliam Museum, Cambridge (MS. 62), and another (now Paris, Bibliothèque Nationale, Lat. 1156 A) for René, her second son. Yet a third work which she ordered from her court painters was probably intended for her eldest son Louis, heir to the Duchy of Anjou and the Kingdom of Sicily after Louis II's death in 1417. This last Book of Hours, a sumptuous production, fit for a king indeed, drew its inspiration (no doubt by her direction) partly from the book illuminated by the brothers Limbourg which she had recently bought. Also to be found in it are details clearly reminiscent of the so-called *Très Riches Heures*, now at Chantilly. That book, the work of those same artists, was never finished, and nothing is known of what became of it between the death of Jean Duc de Berry and the end of the XV Century. But this relationship is a further proof of the interest which the Queen of Sicily took in the art of the brothers Limbourg. So there came to be made, shortly after 1416 and probably about 1418–25, the famous *Heures de Rohan*.

The name by which the book is known calls for some explanation: why 'Rohan', seeing that these *Heures* were made for a member of the family of Anjou? The arms of Rohan that the book carries (in association with other arms never completed) were in fact a later addition. They refer in all probability to Alain IX, Vicomte de Rohan, and to his wife Marie de Lorraine. This Marie, daughter of Antoine de Vaudémont, must presumably have inherited the book from her father. He had defeated René d'Anjou at the battle of Bulgnéville in 1431. René was taken prisoner following the battle, and only regained his liberty by the payment, not finally completed till after 1436, of a heavy ransom. The *Heures*, which had come into his possession after the death in 1434 of his brother and predecessor, Louis, may have formed part of this ransom. In any event, the name *Heures de Rohan*, derived originally from the coat of arms, has stuck, and it is too well known now for a change to be made.

Besides taking as the model for some of their work the *Belles Heures*, the artists of Yolande d'Anjou used also a copy of the *Bible Historiée* in French, illustrated by an Italian. It is still preserved in the Bibliothèque Nationale (Fr. 9561) and there is every reason to think that it was painted for a prince of Anjou and King of Sicily—Louis I, perhaps—and afterwards brought by him to France. Thus with two books from the library of Anjou copied in the *Heures de Rohan* by the artists in Yolande's service, no further proof seems to be needed that these are, by rights, *Heures d'Anjou*.[1]

Yolande's son René was that artist prince to whom we owe more than one masterpiece of French painting, and she had artistic claims in her own right. Was she not a daughter of John I, King of Aragon, who died in 1395, and of Yolande de Bar, daughter of Jean le Bon? Was she not married to Louis II of Anjou in 1400; and was she not, through her father, niece of Martin the Old, the brother of John, and his successor on the throne of Aragon? Both John and Martin of Aragon were lovers of beautiful books. The former had sent him by his mother-in-law, Marie de France, Duchesse de Bar, sister of Charles V, and by his uncles Charles V himself and Jean de Berry, several notable books: a Bible, an Augustine *de Civitate Dei*, a Livy, a copy of the works of Guillaume de Machaut and of Sir John Mandeville; while Martin secured the services of a French illuminator for a number of books, and himself directed, in 1403, the decoration of a magnificent Breviary, a masterpiece of Catalan art (Bibliothèque Nationale, MS. Rothschild 2529). Its calendar reproduces the type of that of the family of Belleville, which was fashionable with several of the princes of Valois: Joan of Navarre, Louis X's daughter; Yolande of Flanders—his daughter-in-law; and later Jean de Berry. Thus Yolande succeeded in discovering a painter of quality and in attaching him to her personal service, and had the ability to select from those of Jean de Berry's books that were sold the most outstanding of all, and to instruct her protégé to base his work on it. She comes before us indeed as one of those rich patrons whose action has been decisive in the life of an artist. We know the work done by the Rohan Master for the family of Anjou, and can compare it with what he did in the period before he belonged to her household. Hitherto the need for earning a living had forced

6

him to devote himself to commercial commissions. It is plain that she gave him the means of realizing himself—of bringing out his own full potentialities—when she took him away from such work, and when she made it possible for him to have the assistance of pupils and associates. Jean de Berry had done the same for the brothers Limbourg. Her son René was ten years old when his mother had the *Heures de Rohan* (as they were later to be called) decorated. If his work shows no trace of the technique of the master who had designed them there may perhaps nevertheless have been even at that time an awakening of the consciousness of his artistic vocation, as the result of his contacts with painting that seems to foreshadow much of what was most personal in René's art: the haunting awareness of the other world, that ever-present sense of death; that same inner vision which René himself was to express in other terms.

Does it not seem probable, indeed, that Yolande's choice of an artist was determined by qualities she found in him answering, maybe, to her own spiritual longings: a deep affinity between the profound and passionate melancholy of the painter and the mood of her own soul—daughter of Aragon that she was? May it not be that, in the cosmopolitan Paris of those days, the artist himself was from Aragon? There is a particular type of figure that haunts his work, thickset, the eyes almond shaped, the eyelids heavy and deepset, the complexion chalky —a type which reminds us of those of the Bolognese painters in the XIV Century and their followers. The painters of northern Spain, and those of Languedoc also, show in this period marked Bolognese inspiration, though it is often given a new character, with a pathos unknown to Italian art of the time, as it is unknown (with these exceptions) in France. We find this characteristic again in missals from Languedoc, or perhaps from Catalonia, one example of which is still preserved among the archives of the house of Aragon, in Barcelona, another almost identical with it at Cambrai (MS. 120). In these, the general manner of the treatment and expression is analogous with those of the Rohan Master; the complexions chalky; the attitudes tense; the faces with their look of profound anguish; bodies naked and emaciated, and even the same background of sky, sprinkled with angels in another shade of the same colour. More distant, but still recognizable links join the *Heures de Rohan* with the already mentioned Breviary of Martin of Aragon, its predecessor by some fifteen years. Even further back, it is to this same Bolognese-Catalan ancestry that we can trace the Pontifical of Pierre de La Jugie, Archbishop of Narbonne (1347–1375), now in Narbonne Cathedral. In default of any written documents, accounts, inventories or contracts, which are rarely found in France for this particular period, it is style which makes possible the establishing of series and sequences, and which gives a greater certainty than iconographical analysis. This style, the result of the apprentice's training and discipline, is handed on from master to pupil through considerable periods. With a process like that of illumination, which becomes more and more of an industry as production becomes increasingly commercial, the mechanics of the craft and the artist's way of handling his materials have a rapidly growing significance. Talent and originality only modify and improve them, bring them to fruition and give them in the process individual character; even originality and talent never free themselves from the technical tradition. Thus for all his originality, the Rohan Master has an ancestry which is clearly marked, with an inherited technique that can never be mistaken for that of artists of truly French descent, nor indeed of Mosan, Rhenish, or Lombard ancestry; whereas a Catalan origin for it is thoroughly credible. On the other hand, the subject matter and also the iconographic type, reveal not only contemporary fashion, but also the taste and direction of a patron; these all enter into the style of the work, which in turn imposes its own hall-mark on them. And while it is true that, in some of its elements, the imagery of the *Heures de Rohan* seems, as has been brilliantly shown, to come from the Rhineland, it does not by any means follow that the Rohan Master was a Rhinelander. Rather, he was one who plunged his hands into that seething Parisian cauldron, into which were poured artistic ideas from all over Europe, and drew out from it what suited his fancy, or that of his patroness Yolande, without feeling on the least degree that he must confine himself to the iconographic conventions of his native land; even supposing that he ever thought much about these conventions or that such distinctions were as sharp as we imagine them today. He drew inspiration from the *Belles Heures*, the work of Mosans who had become French by adoption; also from a historiated Bible painted by an Italian; why may he not then have found it also in Rhenish work? And would it not be natural for a Catalan to enter the household of a princess of Aragon, just as the young Limbourg brothers had found a protector in Philippe le Hardi, whose possessions adjoined their native Guelder, or as certain Lombards were associated with the Italian Christine de Pisan?

*　　*　　*　　*

However that may be (and it cannot be proved one way or the other), the originality of this Master makes it easy to distinguish his hand from that of his Parisian contemporaries, and we have enough from it to be able to reconstruct the broad outlines of his career. The young painter before his work became known, before he surrounded himself with assistants, or set up on his own account and got orders from distinguished patrons or entered their service, began no doubt by working in the workshop of some bookseller or publisher, or in association with one or more colleagues in an *atelier* from which the booksellers commissioned illustrations for their books. The job was distributed among the artists working on it, by quires or by individual leaves, before the manuscript was bound, and the various sections of each copy were thus produced simultaneously. This division of labour can be clearly seen in a number of manuscripts of Parisian origin whose style makes it possible to attribute some of the work to the future Rohan Master. We see him from the very first, from approximately 1405 to 1415, taking a hand in the decoration of secular manuscripts which were much in demand.

They are here enumerated in what must be something like their chronological order:

1. The *Bible Historiale* (not to be confused with the Historiated Bible of Hugues de Saint-Cher). This is a French translation extensively edited, by Guyart Des Moulins, of a Latin commentary on the historical books of the Bible, the original written about 1175 by Pierre le Mangeur (Peter Comestor, *Historia Scholastica*); the commentary is provided with references to secular history. Guyart explains in his preface that he is not presuming to expound any deep biblical mysteries. He leaves this to others more learned than himself. He is confining himself to the insertion into the matter of sacred history, of the main events in pagan history; the expression which he

charmingly uses for this process is 'grafting'. This book, didactic in character and often revised, was widely read, and a number of examples, showing considerable variety in their contents, has survived. One of these was illustrated by the Rohan Master in collaboration with two painters whom we shall often find working with him during the Parisian phase. (^{2}) The first, still at this time a young man, has been given the name 'the Bedford Master', after the Breviary and the magnificent Book of Hours which he painted some fifteen years later for John of Lancaster, Duke of Bedford, Regent of France under the English occupation 1424–1435. The name of the second, like that of the Bedford Master, is unknown. For the sake of simplicity he is here called Master X. The Bedford Master knew how to use colour to convey a plastic feeling, to give the forms in his paintings a roundness without using any tricks of line to do so; he renders this sense of relief by the use of light and shade. He is less aware of space and cannot represent recession in depth, piling up his scenes vertically in the traditional manner. The backgrounds are still screens with diaper pattern, or decorated with foliage scrolls. Landscape does not appear in his work till later. He likes to decorate the margins with tiny pictures which develop, or are comple-mentary to, the main subject. A similar list of idiosyncrasies distinguishes also the Rohan Master in his quite different style; and the parallels between them can be readily understood as between artists working actually on the same manuscripts for a number of years. The Bedford Master decorated other copies of the *Bible Historiale*, in which the hand of the Rohan Master is not to be found. The conclusion may be drawn that he was in charge of an important *atelier*, as his talent might well justify. Master X, one of his associates, is not in his class. He is a conservative, the designs linear and the colours flat.

2. The *Facta et Dicta Memorabilia* of Valerius Maximus, translated at an earlier date into French for Charles V. Here the Rohan Master had the same collaborators, but (in addition to the frontispiece, divided into four compartments) he reserved for himself the majority of the pictures: 85 out of 91. (^{3})

3. The big commercial undertaking of the *atelier* was the illustration of Froissart's *Chronicles*. That famous his-torian died in 1410. We have at least eight copies (^{4}) of the two volumes (not all completed), in which are to be found also the hands of Master X and of others; there were once certainly many more copies now lost. For these large-scale productions the work was divided into approximately equal sections, and labour-saving devices were frankly used. Froissart mentions many battles; which makes it possible to picture repeatedly battle scenes sketched with a rapid brush of metallic blue; hands and faces invisible. But the opening decorations are careful, and each volume has a compartmented frontispiece, sometimes by the Bedford Master, sometimes by the Rohan Master. These semi-luxury books give an excellent notion of the Parisian bookseller's shop of the time, and of the environment in which our artist grew up, before becoming the official painter of Yolande of Anjou. It was a craft becoming increasingly industrialised, closely tied to the actual selling of books. From this milieu there emerged several gifted artists, whose careers were to be made for them by the great collectors.

4. Side by side with history, hunting, and for a start, another of the *atelier's* successful ventures: *Le Livre du Roi Modus et de la Reine Ratio*, a hunting treatise elaborated in the fashion of the age with moral precepts; decorated by the Rohan Master, Master X, and others. (This treatise had first appeared in 1379.) (^{5})

5. Then Gaston Phébus, Count of Foix's *Book of Hunting*. (^{6}) (Of this we possess incidentally a superbly luxur-ious copy, now in the Bibliothèque Nationale, painted by the Bedford Master in his own hand throughout.)

6. In a related *genre*, a treatise of rural and domestic economy by Bartholomew the Englishman, the *de Proprietatibus Rerum*, translated in 1372 by Jean Corbichon for Charles V. (^{7})

7. The series of books decorated by this Bedford-Rohan partnership and their fellows continues with the *De Casibus hominum nobilium ac mulierum* of Boccaccio which Laurent de Premierfait had just translated in 1409. (^{8})

8. And the *De Consolatione philosophiae* of Boethius, followed (9) by the *Game of Chess moralised* and (10) the *Roman de la Rose*. (^{9})

Such were the works in which the future Rohan Master had a hand, working with the Bedford Master and his various assistants. We may add to the list a very effective Hell's Mouth for the Treatise of the Seven Deadly Sins of the Augustinian friar Jacques Legrand, the man who dedicated to Jean de Berry in 1410 his *Book of Good Manners*.[10] This brings more or less

B

to an end the list of the secular work carried out in an *atelier*, which we can associate with the Rohan Master.

*   *   *   *

Perhaps from this time onwards, say about 1405–1415 though it is difficult to be precise, he specialized in Books of Hours. But on them he worked alone; and indeed, no part of the many works of this kind, which he executed before entering the service of the House of Anjou, nor perhaps even afterwards, reveals quite clearly the hand of an associate. The inequalities of style, the difference between one example and another, can be explained by the commercial character of this work also, the degree of finish matching the client's resources; and by the normal development, through some years, of an artist's working life. At all events neither the hand of the Bedford Master (except in one instance where the facts are anyhow uncertain), nor that of Master X, nor of any other of those with whom he was working on secular productions, occurs in these service books. This activity, highly individual, is quite distinct from that which he used to carry on, and perhaps still carried on, in the *atelier* whatever the relations (and here of course we are completely in the dark) between the one and the other. For this class of book he evolves a whole repertory of designs on which he will draw from now onwards to the end, and which he will hand on to his pupils, and to his successors, when they come to continue his work in the West of France, after the years in Anjou that had brought them together under his direction. It is a repertory enriched by his own imaginative powers or by iconography borrowed from other great masters (not only French) who were his rivals, the presentation of which he varies to an almost infinite extent.

The Book of Hours was a concise Breviary for the layman. The 'Little Hours of Our Lady' formed the main part of it, and these were accompanied with offices and prayers varying according to the Use of each diocese or the desires of the customer. Every family had at least one such book. They were handed down from father to son, heirlooms in which generation after generation wrote its own ownership mark; on the fly leaves at the beginning and at the end, notes were sometimes made of significant events in the family history: marriages, births, baptisms, deaths. It was more or less luxurious, according to the money available; bound perhaps in a rich binding, and illustrated with paintings, sometimes by great artists. These paintings occur at the opening of each 'Hour', (Matins, Lauds, Prime and so on) or of the various parts of the book (Office of the Cross, of the Holy Spirit, of the Dead, etc.,), following a general plan which was traditional. Thus the same scenes were repeated from one example to another, to be varied only as cerain themes, or the painter's own ideas (not to mention his talent) developed. Some of the Books of Hours decorated by the Rohan Master, of which at least a dozen are known,[11] follow the Use of Troyes. The record of one Lécuier, illuminator, known to have been established first at Troyes, then at Angers, has been reckoned as fitting these facts, but the dates will not do, and it is simpler to imagine that some bookseller in Troyes gave the artist an order, with a view to selling the finished books in his own part of the country. The remainder follow the Use of Paris. One, now in Lyons, has designs borrowed from the *Belles Heures*, an indication that these were already known to the painter, and that the work is later than Yolande of Aragon's purchase of them, perhaps actually later than the *Heures de Rohan*, or at least not earlier; another, the Balfour Hours, the calendar in which seems to be in the Rohan Master's hand, belongs otherwise to the Boucicaut *atelier*.[12] These complicated interconnections are difficult to unravel, and only detailed comparisons made at great length would bring some order out of the chaos. They might throw some glimmer of light on the Parisian associations of our artist, and so at the same time on the cosmopolitan art of France, Paris being the key to all of it.

We do not know the date at which the Master entered the service of the house of Anjou. On 5th February, 1414, Yolande had left Paris with her daughter Marie, and with Marie's future husband Charles, Comte de Ponthieu, then aged ten, who was one day to be King as Charles VII. After two years at Angers and in Provence, she was once again in Paris with her husband till the death of Jean de Berry on 15th June, 1416; at the end of December the King of Sicily who had been for some time an invalid withdrew from public life; he left Paris, with his wife, for Anjou, where he died on 20th April, 1417.[13] The books executed for her by the Rohan Master and his assistants (the Hours of the younger Yolande, the Hours of René and those called the *Heures de Rohan*) follow the Use of Paris, not that of Angers. But the precise Use may be of secondary importance for a family which divided its time between Paris and its estates in the provinces. We have every reason to believe that the *Heures de Rohan* are the latest of the group. And so we may be disposed to agree that our painter, being a Parisian, must have been engaged by the Queen of Sicily before she left Paris in February 1414, though it does not follow that he went with her himself to Angers. The Hours now at Cambridge of the younger Yolande, her daughter, carry in the margin, besides a series of designs drawn from a then fashionable text (the *Pilgrimage* of Guillaume de Digulleville), a complete Apocalypse, which it would be interesting to compare with the famous tapestries ordered by Louis I, father-in-law of Queen Yolande.

From the moment when he began to work for the family of Anjou, more precisely for Yolande and her children, the Rohan Master becomes almost a different man. He had at first worked as an assistant in the workshop of the Bedford Master and his associates (including Master X). He had subsequently become an independent producer of Books of Hours, and these two activities may have overlapped. Now we find him at the head of his own workshop. He has with him assistants, none of whom can be recognized as having been a former colleague. It is a new personnel, very close to him in ideas and in technique, far removed from him in talent, in which it is often enormously inferior. This means of course a group of pupils, or at least of subordinates, which he forms and shapes to his wishes. He has now the possibility of giving himself as it were another pair of hands; and he takes it. Thus there are serious difficulties in distinguishing what work in this phase belongs precisely to him or what to the most gifted of his assistants. The *atelier*, if it leaves indeed some scope for individual craftsmanship, keeps a certain overall unity under the direction of the master, who undoubtedly plans all the

work, and carries it through to the stage of the actual drawings. We have agreed that his connec-
tion with the house of Anjou began in 1414, that during the following formative years he
worked still in Paris; but at some moment this *atelier de Rohan* must have moved to Angers.
This must be the explanation why the latest in date of his works follows the Use of Angers[14];
and why so many Books of Hours of the mid-century, latest representatives of the school, be-
long to Western France and Brittany[15]: the Hours of Jean de Montauban, admiral of France,
husband of Anna de Kéranrais; Hours of the Use of Nantes made for Pierre II, Duc de
Bretagne; Hours of Françoise de Dinan, sister-in-law of François Duc de Bretagne; Hours of
Isabella Stuart, his wife; and also a copy of the *Somme le Roy*, by Brother Lawrence, decorated
for the same Isabella Stuart.

*　　*　　*　　*

The *Heures de Rohan* from which eight of the finest designs are here reproduced, have been
reckoned among the masterpieces of medieval art ever since Emile Mâle demonstrated their
quality at the time of the 1904 exhibition of French Primitives in Paris. If the conclusions here
put forward are accepted, these masterpieces can now be dated to approximately the year 1418
(the limits in either direction being 1416 and 1420–1425) and can be shown to have been
executed in Paris for Yolande of Aragon, Duchess of Anjou and Queen of Sicily, by a painter
who perhaps came from Catalonia. But his artistic education was in a Parisian *atelier*, and he
was helped by assistants working under his direction and trained in his technique.

That technique was traditional through and through. The Rohan Master was no innovator.
He derives from his personal temperament, and perhaps from his regional origins, a melancholy
and anguish which make him the antithesis of his Parisian colleagues, with their gaiety, and
their care-free eagerness for what is new. Like the most brilliant of them he becomes a court
painter, but unlike them, he does not change his coat to become a courtier. With him there is
nothing comparable to such a change as that of the brothers Limbourg, which comes out so
clearly in the contrast between the *Belles Heures* and the *Très Riches Heures*, (despite the outstanding genius of the latter). About him there is nothing of the Boucicaut or the Bedford
Masters, for their sumptuous productions betray the need for concessions to the taste of their
elegant and wealthy patrons. He reaches the summit of his achievement in being himself; and
if sometimes he seems at first sight to try to attach himself to the fashion of his time, his indifference to it and the excess of his own feelings prevent him from understanding it. His melancholy is a tortured obsession with the drama of life and death playing itself out daily before his
eyes, and this finds expression in the features, the attitudes, even in the size, of the figures he
paints: the bodies are hunched forward, leaning downwards, for all the world as if they were
weighed down by some mysterious threat; the corpses, elongated and emaciated, the flesh pale
as wax. His vision of the human body fluctuates between two extremes. There is not one of his
characters who has not something that marks the curse of nature which overwhelms humanity.
It is only the look of the heavenly Father that is serene. Its beauty has a divine calm, and is free

from that human restlessness. And no other painter, not even the brothers Limbourg, could give to the Virgin, to the triumphant mother of God Himself, that youthful peace or that lambent spirituality and innocence which make the Rohan Master's madonnas the loveliest in medieval French art. From the corpulent peasant with his coarse features and clumsy build (Pl. 4) to the idealized representations of the Mother of Christ (Pls. 5 and 6), he creates an entire range of attitudes and expression, unrivalled in its variety. Like the Bedford Master and, perhaps thanks to him, if indeed it is true that they worked side by side in the same *atelier*, he is not only a draughtsman but in a true sense a painter; he uses colours to model the features with greater subtlety, and there is, in this kind of work, nothing to equal the refinement and delicacy of some of the features or draperies, where the lightest touch of the brush is enough to suggest relief or to indicate its depth. The tortured visionary is at one and the same time also an extremely conscientious craftsman. It does not matter that the finish is uneven, that on one scene more time and care are spent than on another. We must not be too hasty in limiting his share, in the works painted at the height of his career, to only a few pages; and this specially applies to the *Heures de Rohan*. In fact the work is almost all his own. He leaves to his assistants the general composition of hardly any scene whatever, and for the most part only the job of finishing with a touch here and colour there. This is noticeable in marginal designs of the calendar, where apart from some which have quite clearly been carried out by apprentices, there is nothing to distinguish them from the secular illustrations that he used to paint in the *atelier* of the Bedford Master, or for his own Books of Hours painted for the market. It must be insisted that the *atelier* of the Rohan Master formed round him, under his inspiration, only after he had begun to work for the house of Anjou. The point needs emphasis once again, for in no other way can this artist's career be explained. He did not find a group of assistants ready made for him, some group in which thanks to some existing affinity with him he might by a miracle develop his qualities. It was he who created it, in response to Queen Yolande's commissions, and in order to carry them out.

That he learnt from the Bedford Master, even if eventually he left him behind, can be seen (as suggested above) in his taste for marginal decorations—though these form, with him, distinct cycles and are not complementary to the main design; also from those round, chubby faces used particularly for angels, and so different from the other types to which the Rohan Master has accustomed us. These angel faces imitate a pattern used indiscriminately by the Bedford Master in his work; and in putting these faces on to every sort of character he shows the comparative lack of tact which distinguishes his work from that of the Rohan Master.

The living body interests the Rohan Master. His nudes are excellent. He is supremely good in representing the mood, whether the subject is divine or human, by facial expression, attitude or gesture. But while, like the Bedford Master, he has a plastic sense, he also, like that Master in the earlier work, does not understand space, depth, or perspective; and this is a calculated neglect. Completely indifferent to logic in this sphere, he plants down some miscellaneous architectural fragments against a background uniformly made up of screens decorated with diaper patterns or scrolls of foliage. The scene interests him, but the surroundings not at all; we do not find landscapes in his work except for an altogether summary treatment, while his rivals were

13

little by little beginning to portray country, to explore the horizon and to discover the different moods of the sky. For him the sky is no more than a screen embroidered with angels in shades of the same colour, or strewed with wings, or symmetrical golden clouds. The time of the Van Eycks is not far off. But the Rohan Master is blind to the coming revelation. He paints ideas, and is without a thought for that conquest of the external world which is beginning to assert itself. In the full tide of the European Gothic movement, he is the last representative of the Romanesque spirit.

PLATE 1

THE CRUCIFIXION

This miniature stands at the opening of a section of St John's account of the Passion. The Master has reproduced in it (with only slight modifications) a Crucifixion in the *Bible Historiée*, illuminated by an Italian; a book which his assistants used as a model in the marginal decoration in the *Heures*. While it is a close reproduction of the original, the painter keeps the characteristics which mark his personality so strongly. The design is borrowed, but the formal expression is his own, and in following his Italian model in detail, he does not modify his style in any way. We find here, even in the detail, the technique already characteristic of the work done before he entered the service of the house of Anjou. It is the technique already to be seen in his early service books made for the Parisian market.

On either side of the crucified Christ, the two thieves; left, the good thief, left above him St Michael, who catches up his soul (in the traditional form of a naked infant) and pierces through a devil with his spear. Right the unrepentant thief, his soul snatched away by another devil. The legs of the thieves are broken (cf. St John XIX, 32). At the foot of the cross a group of soldiers, mounted on horses, carrying lances with pennons; in the foreground on the left, Joseph of Arimathea, also mounted, and apparently being addressed by the Virgin and St John. Behind the two latter, three women (of one only part of the halo is visible): Mary of Magdala, Mary the mother of James and John, and the mother of Zebedee. The sky is dark and sombre, dotted with stars, and thronged with angels robed in its own dark colour.

PLATE 2

THE ANNUNCIATION

Here the theme is again treated in the Italian manner. The Virgin is seated, her back to the spectator, facing three quarters to the left; beyond her, a desk with books on it shows that she is in her oratory. Gabriel enters and kneels to her, saying the words AVE GRATIA PLENA DOMINUS TECUM (on the scroll which he holds). Below, on the right, Isaiah, who points with his finger at a scroll held in his left hand with the prophetic words ECCE VIRGO CONCIPIET (Is. VII, 4); thus the Old Testament is fulfilled in the New. In the top left hand corner, God the Father looks down; He is nimbed with a cruciform halo, to indicate that this is also Christ, for in this figure two persons of the Trinity are united in one; while the Holy Spirit in the form of a dove descends, followed by two angels, in rays of light. This light symbolizes the Virgin conception; the light makes the glass through which it shines glow, without breaking it. In the margin, angels carrying scrolls on which are inscribed the words of Isaiah's prophecy.

The ground is covered with a pattern of cubes; it is piled up vertically (though the painter has attempted to represent it in perspective) to the line where it meets the sky; which is blue with a scattering of golden cloudlets. The same unsuccessful attempt to render perspective is seen in the architectural setting. The spindly columns indeed diminish in thickness with the distance, and the vaulting of the roof in the background is lower; similar features appear in the chair on which the Virgin is seated. The general effect however is over-elaborate to the point of confusion; the Master is here imitating motifs of which his former collaborators had made skilful use, but he here misunderstands them. The angels at the top of the columns are derived ultimately (by way of the *Belles Heures* of Jean de Berry) from those inhabited niches, surmounting capitals, of which the idea first appears in the architecture of Milan Cathedral (between 1386 and 1390). In the Rohan Master's version it is no longer functional and has lost its meaning.

The painting illustrates the Office of Matins.

PLATE 3

THE VISITATION

The Virgin, St Elizabeth, and Zacharias. The design has a marvellous balance. It is a decoration admirably planned so that all its main lines should meet in the figure of the Virgin. She stands with her back to a rock crowned with a tree the line of which emphasizes her standing figure. Above, like a canopy, a group of angels. The wings of some of them frame her head. The kneeling angel (the same figure as in the Annunciation), serves also to complete the frame of her tall figure; though on the extreme left, this is in fact the most crowded section of the design. The artist whose perspective, and whose sense of the third dimension of space, is indifferent, shows here a superb appreciation of composition.

The painting illustrates the Office of Lauds.

PLATE 4

THE ANNOUNCEMENT TO THE SHEPHERDS

This scene, preceding the Office of Terce, is here substantially modified from the traditional representation. Normally the shepherds are taken by surprise at the heavenly message with its astonishing tidings, and are rooted to the ground, faces gazing up towards the sky. Here the design expresses joy ("*Evangelizo vobis gaudium magnum,*" Luke II, 10), a joy that is, however, serious, and profound. As it lays hold of the shepherds, it makes the stout old peasant with his portly figure dance to the sound of his own pipe, in spite of his size and his huge and heavy boots. Near him a peasant woman is milking a sheep. Neither seems to listen to the angels in the sky; only the traditional sheepdog marks their presence, barking at this strange visitation. Though normally the interest of the design is built up to these angels (who are after all the most important feature of the story) and every movement is directed on them, it is here the dancer who occupies the foreground, and his great size dominates the design, claiming some third of it for himself. And it is the dance here which is significant; but the joy is nevertheless something solemn, and it does not interrupt the day's jobs waiting to be done; it suggests nothing in the least like gaiety, in the huge figure which embodies it. The woman is copied from the calendar of the *Très Riches Heures* of Jean de Berry. The dancing figure comes from some marginal decoration.

PLATE 5

THE PURIFICATION

Nothing shows better than this picture the artist's complete indifference to realism. The design is crowded with architectural motifs, disparate in character; it is concerned not with representing, but rather with suggesting the temple building, both exterior and interior, by the silhouette (against a sky sprinkled with stars and cloudlets), which shows a series of turrets heaped together on no rational plan. This is a formula, complicated and confused in this version, which appears for instance in the mosaics of Sta. Maria Maggiore in Rome, San Vitale in Ravenna, and the illuminations of the Tours Pentateuch. After eight centuries, similar conditions were producing similar results. Below, to the left, the city wall of Jerusalem, with a gate and a well; the outside of the temple is in part shown, in part the inside, opened however to show the actual scene of the Presentation. Thus the Virgin is inside and outside the Temple, at one and the same time; she is both behind the city wall and far in front of it. On the left, two women, of whom one is carrying doves in a basket.

Illustrating the Office of None.

PLATE 6

FLIGHT INTO EGYPT

The Holy Family is on the way to Egypt, Mary seated on a mule led by a youthful figure, Joseph bringing up the rear of the little procession. The scene takes up the whole width of the page, and its scale is larger (although in fact it is in the background) than that of the foreground, where some of Herod's lancers, sent to catch the fugitives, are questioning peasants who are reaping. The two registers are separated by rocks on which trees are growing; the setting is like the wings of a stage, and it recalls the technique of Carolingian painting, derived in turn from antique originals. The horseman in the foreground comes from the *Très Riches Heures*, like the peasant woman in Pl. 4. The treatment as a whole is quite unrealistic, though there is notable realism in the details if they are separately regarded. The miniature stands at the opening of Vespers.

PLATE 7

PIETA

The Virgin sinks forward over the body of Christ, her arms outstretched towards it, her body supported by the arms of St John. Christ's body lies stretched on the ground, naked, at the foot of a cross so slender that it can be a symbol only of the actual instrument of His torture. In the sky above, to the right, God the Father. Like the Son, He wears a cruciform halo; He lifts His hand in blessing. John can only with difficulty hold up the Virgin's body, fainting as she is with grief. He has to steady himself with his right foot, the tip of which is just visible. He turns towards the Almighty with a strange, almost violent movement of the head, as if reproaching the Father with His hardness of heart towards His Son. Wings of gold make a sort of curtain, fluttering stormily in the sky which is strewn with stars. The group formed by the Virgin and St John is in essence a long diagonal dividing the lower right hand corner of the picture. It rises gently, then is broken off along the line of the Virgin's right arm and turns downward suddenly to the left. Nowhere more splendidly than in this design has the Master conveyed the sense of passion by the eloquence of his line, by the emphasis on physical details, and by the calculated distortion of the figures. The scene comes at the opening of the Hours of the Cross.

PLATE 8

THE DEAD BEFORE HIS JUDGE

The dead man lies stretched out on a cloth, coloured in warm colours, which by contrast relieve the pallor of the emaciated body. The ground below is scattered with bones. The corpse is naked, for we take nothing out of this world; we are then nothing but ourselves, without even a covering to help us. From his mouth there comes a scroll which bears the words of Ps. XXX, v. 6: IN MANUS TUAS, DOMINE, COMMENDO SPIRITUM MEUM. REDEM-ISTI ME, DOMINE DEUS VERITATIS. From the sky above, the Lord, represented overwhelmingly large in scale, is looking down on the body: the expression is of contemplative seriousness, the head inclined forward in a movement full of pity and tenderness. The hair and long beard are white; He is the Father, but also the Son, as is shown by the cruciform halo which bears the words JESUS NAZARENUS REX JUDAEORUM. He is Lord of this world for in His left hand He carries the orb, and in His right the sword of justice. Jesus, who has power to forgive sins and to judge, is God, as is the Father. He is answering to the dead man: 'Do penitence for thy sins; in the judgement thou shalt be with me.' In the sky which is strewn with stars and with golden angels, the devil has secured the soul of the dead man, repre-sented in the form of a naked child; but the Archangel Michael hurls himself down with lifted sword to attack the devil, whom he seizes by the hair, and who is pierced by spears held by war-riors of the heavenly host. This struggle for the possession of the soul is a traditional theme. But the mighty figure of the Father is this artist's own; and he has given it a majestic gentleness and serene power, which are in complete contrast with the withered rigidity and the horrifyingly distorted limbs of the dead body. So the design consists basically of contrasting bands; one is that of life and light; the other is that of earth and of death.

The painting stands before the Office of the Dead.

NOTES

[1] On the *Heures de Rohan* in general (Bibliothèque Nationale, Lat. 9471), see: V. Leroquais, *Les Livres d'heures manuscrits de la Bibliothèque Nationale*, 1927, Vol. I, p. 281; Ad. Heimann, 'Der Meister der "Grandes Heures de Rohan" und seine Werkstatt', in *Städel Jahrbuch*, VII/VIII, 1932, p. 1; J. Porcher, 'Two Models for the "Heures de Rohan"' in the *Journal of the Warburg and Courtauld Institutes*, VIII, 1945, p. 1.

[2] Bibliothèque Nationale, Fr. 15393–15394. A copy in Brussels (Bibliothèque Royale, 9004) has a frontispiece by the Bedford Master, but contains no work by the Master of Rohan.

[3] Bibliothèque Nationale, Fr. 20320.

[4] Bibliothèque Nationale, Fr. 2662; 2663–2664; 2675–2676; Brussels, Bibliothèque Royale, II, 88; Stonyhurst College, MS. I (information from Prof. O. Pächt); Toulouse, MS. 511; MS. sold at Sotheby's, London, 6th December, 1954, No. 43; also No. 8 in Catalogue No. 57 of P. Bérès, Paris, 1958.

[5] Bibliothèque Nationale, Fr. 1302; Vienna, Nationalbibliothek, MS. 2573 (see C. Nordenfalk, *Kung Praktiks och drottning Teoris jaktbok*, 1955, pp. 39, 47, 94).

[6] Dresden, Saxony, Landesbibliothek, Oc. 61 (L. Olschki, *Manuscrits français à peintures des Bibliothèques d'Allemagne*, Geneva, 1932, plate XVI; R. Bruck, *Die Malereien in den Handschriften des Königreichs Sachsen*, Dresden 1906, figs. 152–154).

[7] Bibliothèque Nationale, Fr. 2253/1.

[8] Bibliothèque Nationale, Fr. 226; Fr. 16995.

[9] Bibliothèque Nationale, Fr. 812.

[10] Bibliothèque Nationale, Lat. 14245.

[11] Sainte-Geneviève, MS. 1278; Arsenal, MS. 647 and Princeton University Library, Garrett 48 (E. Panofsky, in *Medieval Studies in Memory of A. Kingsley Porter*, 1939, II, p. 479); Amiens, MS. Lescalopier 17; Harvard University Library, Richardson 42 (E. Panofsky, 'The de Buz Book of Hours', in *Harvard Library Bulletin*. III, 1949, p. 163); Coll. H. Eisemann (The Walters Art Gallery, *Illuminated Books of the Middle Ages and Renaissance*, 1949, No. 98); Coll. Lee of Fareham (Ad. Heimann, in *Burlington Magazine*, August 1937, p. 83); Chantilly, Musée Condé, MS. 67; Coll. David McC. McKell (information from Prof. O. Pächt); British Museum, Harl. 2934 (information from Prof. Francis Wormald); Victoria and Albert Museum, G. Reid No. 4; Lyons MS. 5140; Bibliothèque Nationale, Lat. 13262; Oxford, Bodleian Library, Buchanan E.9. (information from Prof. O. Pächt). See also Catal. Boerner, 28th November, 1912; Sotheby's sale of 28th June, 1948, No. 219.

[12] London, private collection (information from Dr. Rosy Schilling). The so-called Boucicaut Master worked for a long period with the Bedford Master.

[13] G. Du Fresne de Beaucourt, *Histoire de Charles VII*, 1882, t.l. p. 16.

[14] Formerly in the Martin-Le Roy collection, Paris.

[15] Bibliothèque Nationale, *Les Manuscrits à peintures en France du XIIIᵉ au XVIᵉ siècle*, 1955, Nos. 236 to 240.